COOKING FOR YOUR CAT

HEALTHY HOMEMADE KITTY CUISINE SEASONED WITH AFFECTION

Sophie Klein

Parragon

Bath New York Singapore Hong Kong Cologne Delhi Melbourne

All the recipes in this book have been carefully researched and formulated, and have been tried out on various cats. However, we cannot rule out the possibility of particular food intolerances in certain cats. The publisher and the author cannot be held liable in this case.

The recipes are intended for special occasions; in other words, they are meant to be used as an addition to your cat's regular diet. They cannot and should not replace a proper balanced diet. If you are uncertain about your cat's tolerance of an ingredient or preparation method, please consult your vet. With very young cats, pregnant cats, sick cats, and cats that have to keep to a particular diet, it is essential to ask the advice of your vet before feeding them homemade food.

Not everything that people like to eat is good for cats. Alcohol, cocoa, chocolate, raw pork (including raw ham and salami), avocado, onions, garlic, strong spices, sugar, and excessive salt are all known to be harmful. This list does not claim to be comprehensive.

This is a Parragon Publishing Book
This edition published in 2010
Parragon Publishing, Queen Street House, 4 Queen Street,
Bath BA1 1HE, UK

German edition produced by
Production: ditter.projektagentur GmbH; **Project coordination:** Michael Ditter; **Food photography:** Jo Kirchherr; **Home economist:** Sonja Schubert; **Illustrations:** Kyra Stempell; **Editing:** Sebnem Yavuz; **Design:** Sabine Vonderstein; **Lithography:** Klaussner Medien Service GmbH

English-language edition produced by
Cambridge Publishing Management Ltd
Translator: Jackie Smith

The publisher wishes to express particular thanks to Dr. Burton Miller, renowned holistic doctor of veterinary medicine, for his careful advice on the recipes included in this book. Based in Huntington, NY, Dr. Miller is the founder of the Animal Wellness Center (www.animalwellness.net).

This book uses imperial, metric, and US cup measurements. Follow the same units of measurement throughout; do not mix imperial and metric. All spoon measurements are level: teaspoons are assumed to be 5 ml, and tablespoons are assumed to be 15 ml. Unless otherwise stated, milk is assumed to be whole, and eggs and individual vegetables such as potatoes are medium.

ISBN: 978-1-4075-8078-4

Printed in China

Contents

Foreword

Cats are connoisseurs. Unlike dogs, they tend to be very fussy and whimsical, not just about their food. If their normal feeding routines are disturbed or their menu changes dramatically, they soon become moody and reject unfamiliar food. Cats are also curious, though; if you leave them in peace and give them time, they will eventually embark on a cautious investigation of the contents of their food bowl, before enjoying the tasty new morsels you have served.

My cat always used to rub affectionately around my legs when I was preparing all kinds of tasty dishes for myself and my guests. It was this that caused me to set aside a small portion of the ingredients during preparation, so that I could cook up a cat's dinner in a separate pan for my four-legged friend. For example, "Lucca's favorite risotto" was derived from an asparagus risotto with grilled chicken breast cooked for human consumption, while the minced meat for our own meatballs was transformed, with the addition of some cheese, rolled oats, and egg, into "Lady's cheese balls."

So after a time I had assembled a whole collection of recipes for little dishes for cats—which is what formed the basis for this cookbook. The dishes are easy to prepare, and have been tested on many occasions by my cat Paula and her friends. However, the recipes are meant as gourmet treats for special occasions, and are not intended to take the place of a cat's regular daily diet. I serve up these dishes twice a week at most, to supplement my cat's diet or as a reward. If you want to feed your cat only homemade food, it is important to seek the advice of a vet beforehand, and to find out about the essential components of a healthy feline diet. My recipes are not suitable for cats that are ill or that have to follow a particular diet.

When cooking for healthy cats, there are still certain rules that must be adhered to. Not everything that people like to eat is good for cats. Alcohol, cocoa, chocolate, raw pork (including raw ham and salami), avocado, onions, garlic, strong spices, sugar, and excessive salt are definitely known to be harmful. Rice, potatoes, pasta, fish, and poultry must only be given cooked, and no bones (meat or fish) should ever be put in kitty's bowl. Please soak cereal flakes and grains to soften them before feeding to your cat, and finely chop or grate vegetables. Artificial colorings and flavorings must be avoided.

If, despite all the loving care you put into cooking it, your kitty leaves its meal untouched, do not be disappointed, and whatever happens do not let your furry friend go hungry as a punishment. Just try again another day with a different recipe. Every cat has its own preferences. My Paula feasted on the fish dishes, and the chicken chips and fish munchies, with particular enthusiasm. The many other grateful taste-testers also voiced their approval with contented purring. Paula and I would like to take this opportunity to thank them and their owners once again.

Sophie Klein

FOR SOUP LOVERS

Classic chicken soup

Makes 2 to 3 portions

For the chicken stock:
4 cups (1 L) water
¼ tsp salt
2 skinless chicken thighs
2 carrots, peeled and diced
1 cup (100 g) celery stalk, washed and diced

For the soup:
¾ oz (20 g) carrot
1 tsp vegetable oil
1 tbsp (10 g) cooked rice
½ tsp freshly chopped flat-leaf parsley

For the chicken stock, bring the water to a boil in a saucepan with the salt, and add the chicken thighs and the vegetables. Simmer covered for 45 minutes, remove from the heat, and allow to cool.

Remove the chicken thighs from the stock and take the meat off the bones. Discard the bones. Strain the stock into a bowl and discard the vegetables. Measure out 3½ fl oz (100 ml) stock and 3½ oz (100 g) chicken for the chicken soup, and put to one side. The remaining stock and chicken can be used for other dishes or frozen.

For the soup, peel and grate the carrot. Heat the oil in a saucepan, and sauté the rice and grated carrot. Pour in the measured quantity of stock, bring to a boil and simmer for ten minutes.

Meanwhile, finely chop the weighed-out chicken. Remove the soup from the heat. Add the chicken and parsley, and allow to cool to room temperature. Serve a portion at a time.

Fish soup for Chico

Makes 2 to 3 portions

1½ oz (40 g) salmon fillet, skinless and boneless
1½ oz (40 g) mackerel fillet, skinless and boneless
¾ oz (20 g) raw shrimps, peeled
¾ oz (20 g) zucchini
1 tsp sunflower oil
½ cup (100 ml) water
½ tsp flaked tuna
⅛ oz (5 g) dried soup pasta
½ tsp freshly chopped flat-leaf parsley

Cut all the fish into small cubes. Cut the shrimps up small. Finely dice the zucchini.

Heat the oil in a saucepan and sauté the diced zucchini. Add the water, the flaked tuna, and the soup pasta. Bring to a boil and simmer for ten minutes.

Add the fish cubes and shrimps to the soup and simmer on a low heat for ten minutes until cooked through. Remove the soup from the heat and allow to cool. Stir in the parsley. Serve a portion at a time.

Beef pot for Tiger

Makes 2 to 3 portions

3½ oz (100 g) beef
1 tsp sunflower oil
½ cup (100 ml) water
¼ oz (10 g) potato
¼ oz (10 g) green beans
¼ tsp additive-free vegetable stock powder
½ tsp freshly chopped flat-leaf parsley

Cut the beef into very small pieces. Heat the sunflower oil in a saucepan and brown the meat. Add the water and cook, covered, for 20 minutes.

Meanwhile, peel and finely grate the potato. Wash and trim the beans, and chop them finely. Add the grated potato, beans, and stock powder to the meat. Simmer these together for a further 15 minutes.

Remove from the heat and allow to cool. Stir in the chopped parsley. Serve a portion at a time.

Liver dumpling soup

Makes 2 to 3 portions

1 egg yolk
⅛ cup (10 g) instant rolled oats
2½ oz (70 g) ground beef
1 oz (30 g) beef liver, puréed
½ tsp freshly chopped flat-leaf parsley
⅛ oz (5 g) carrot, peeled
⅛ oz (5 g) celery stalk
1 cup (250 ml) water
¼ tsp additive-free vegetable stock powder

Whisk the egg yolk in a bowl, stir in the rolled oats, and leave to soak for ten minutes.

Add the ground beef, puréed beef liver, and parsley. Knead these together. With damp hands, shape the beef mixture into small balls.

Finely grate the carrot and celery. Put the water in a saucepan with the vegetables and stock powder, and bring to the boil. Add the meatballs and cook for ten minutes on a low heat.

Remove the soup from the heat and allow to cool. Serve a portion at a time of the liver dumplings, along with a little of the liquid.

HEARTY MEALS

Turkey strips

Makes 2 to 3 portions

3½ oz (100 g) turkey breast, skinless
1 tsp sesame oil
2 tbsp water
1 tbsp (10 g) cooked rice
1 tbsp cream
¼ oz (10 g) alfalfa sprouts, finely chopped
½ tsp dried coconut

Cut the turkey breast into thin strips. Heat the sesame oil in a saucepan, sauté the turkey breast strips, add two tablespoons of water, and cook for ten minutes.

Remove the pan from the heat and allow to cool. Mix in the rice, cream, alfalfa sprouts, and dried coconut. Serve a portion at a time.

Sally's favorite fish

Makes 2 to 3 portions

3½ oz (100 g) salmon fillet, skinned and boned
1 tsp olive oil
2 tbsp (25 ml) water
¼ cup (15 g) spinach, finely chopped
¼ oz (10 g) chopped cooked noodles
1 tbsp sour cream

Cut the salmon into very small cubes. Heat the oil in a saucepan and sauté the salmon. Add two tablespoons of water, the spinach, and the noodles, and cook for ten minutes.

Remove the pan from the heat and allow to cool.
Gently stir in the sour cream. Serve a portion at a time.

Lady's cheese balls

Makes 2 to 3 portions

1 egg yolk
1 tbsp instant rolled oats
½ oz (15 g) peeled, cooked pumpkin
2¾ oz (80 g) ground beef
½ tsp freshly chopped flat-leaf parsley
¾ oz (20 g) mozzarella cheese
1 tsp vegetable oil

Whisk the egg yolk in a bowl, stir in the rolled oats, and leave to soak for ten minutes.

Finely dice the pumpkin. Add it to the rolled oats and egg mixture, together with the ground beef and parsley, and knead.

Cut the mozzarella into three slices and shape the meat mixture into six meatballs. Sandwich each slice of mozzarella between two meatballs and flatten down slightly.

Heat the oil in a frying pan and fry the meatballs on a medium heat for three minutes on each side.

Remove from the pan and leave to cool. Serve a portion at a time, cut into manageable-sized pieces.

Casserole with heart

Makes 2 to 3 portions

2½ oz (70 g) chicken breast fillet, skinless
1 oz (30 g) chicken hearts
½ cup (150 ml) water
1 tsp butter
1 tsp flour
1 tbsp cream
1 tbsp grated cheese
½ oz (15 g) Boston lettuce
1 tbsp (10 g) cooked rice

Put the chicken breast fillet and chicken hearts in a saucepan with the water. Bring to a boil and cook for 15 minutes. Drain the meat, reserving the cooking liquid. Allow the meat to cool, and cut into small pieces.

Melt the butter in a small saucepan, stir in the flour, and cook for a short time. Add ¼ cup of the cooking liquid plus the cream, and bring to the boil. Stir in the cheese so it melts into the sauce. Remove the saucepan from the heat and allow to cool.

Wash the Boston lettuce and finely chop. Mix the rice, meat and Boston lettuce with the sauce. Serve a portion at a time.

Leroy's liver stew

Makes 2 to 3 portions

3½ oz (100 g) beef liver
1 tsp sunflower oil
¼ cup (50 ml) water
½ oz (15 g) peeled, cooked potato
1 tbsp sour cream
1 tsp freshly chopped flat-leaf parsley

Wash the beef liver, pat it dry, and cut it into small cubes. Heat the oil in a saucepan, add the cubes of liver and brown. Add the water and cook for ten minutes on a medium heat.

Mash the potato with a fork; then mix it into the liver stew, together with the sour cream and parsley. Allow to cool. Serve a portion at a time.

Paula's stir-fried fish

Makes 2 to 3 portions

3½ oz (100 g) mackerel fillet, skinned and boned
¾ oz (10 g) zucchini
1 tsp olive oil
2 tsp tomato paste
2 tbsp water
1 tbsp (10 g) cooked rice
2 tsp cream
½ tsp freshly chopped basil

Cut the mackerel fillet into small cubes. Finely grate the zucchini.

Heat the oil in a frying pan and stir-fry the fish and zucchini on a medium heat. Add the tomato paste, the water, and the rice to the pan. Simmer for ten minutes.

Remove from the heat and allow to cool. Mix in the cream and basil. Serve a portion at a time.

Lamb hotpot with carrot

Makes 2 to 3 portions

3½ oz (100 g) lamb
¾ oz (20 g) carrot
1 tsp olive oil
2 tbsp water
1 tbsp plain yogurt
½ tsp freshly chopped flat-leaf parsley

Cut the lamb into small cubes. Peel and finely grate the carrot.

Heat the olive oil in a frying pan and brown the meat on all sides. Add the grated carrot, followed by the water. Cook on a medium heat for ten minutes. Remove from the heat and allow to cool.

Mix in the yogurt and parsley. Serve a portion at a time.

ITALIAN
FOR TIGERS

Vitello tonnato

Makes 2 to 3 portions

2 oz (60 g) veal cutlet
1 tsp olive oil
2 tbsp water
1 anchovy fillet in oil
1½ oz (40 g) canned tuna in brine, drained
2 tbsp plain yogurt
½ tsp freshly chopped basil

Beat the veal cutlet very flat. Heat the oil in a frying pan and fry the meat for one minute on each side. Remove it from the pan, allow to cool, and cut into small pieces.

Loosen the pan residues with the water and allow to cool. Rinse off the anchovy fillet, pat it dry, place it in a blender together with the tuna, yogurt, and pan residues, and purée them. Mix the basil into the sauce.

Serve the pieces of meat with the tuna sauce, a portion at a time.

Carpaccio Caruso

Makes 1 portion

1½ oz (40 g) very fresh raw beef
1 tsp (5 g) mixed salad leaves (e.g. arugula, Boston lettuce)
½ tsp olive oil
1 tbsp water
¼ tsp grated Parmesan

Cut the meat into very thin strips, flatten them slightly with the back of a knife, and arrange on a plate.

Finely chop the salad leaves. In a bowl, mix the olive oil with the water to make a dressing, and mix with the chopped salad leaves.

Sprinkle it over the meat and scatter the Parmesan on top. Serve immediately.

Tip
Many cats see raw meat as prey that first has to be captured and killed. In this case, to avoid a lot of mess around the house, the carpaccio should be served outside. Alternatively, ground beef can be used, mixed with the salad leaves and the Parmesan.

Bolognese à la "Nero"

Makes 2 to 3 portions

¼ oz (10 g) carrot, peeled
⅛ oz (5 g) celery stalk
1 tsp olive oil
3½ oz (100 g) ground beef
2 tsp tomato paste
¼ cup water
¼ oz (10 g) chopped cooked pasta
1 tsp grated Parmesan

Grate the carrot and finely chop the celery.

Heat the olive oil in a saucepan and fry the ground beef until crumbly. Add the vegetables and tomato paste, and cook for a short time. Pour in the water and cook for a further ten minutes.

Mix the Bolognese sauce with the pasta and allow to cool. Scatter the Parmesan on top, and serve a portion at a time.

Lucca's favorite risotto

Makes 2 to 3 portions

3½ oz (100 g) chicken breast fillet, skinless
½ oz (15 g) green asparagus
1 tsp olive oil
¼ oz (10 g) risotto rice
5 tbsp (75 l) homemade chicken stock, see p. 8 (alternatively, dissolve ¼ tsp additive-free vegetable stock powder in 5 tbsp (75 ml) water)
¼ tsp butter
1 tsp grated Parmesan

Cut the chicken breast fillet into small cubes. Finely chop the asparagus.

Heat the olive oil in a saucepan and sauté the cubes of meat. Add the rice and asparagus, and sauté briefly. Add two tablespoons of the stock and continue stirring until the liquid has almost evaporated. Add the rest of the stock and cook uncovered on a low heat for 15 minutes, stirring occasionally.

Remove the risotto from the heat, stir in the butter and Parmesan, and allow to cool. Serve a portion at a time.

FRITTATA FOR MIDGE

Makes 2 to 3 portions

1¾ oz (50 g) cooked shrimps (without preservatives)
1 egg
2 tbsp low-fat cream cheese
½ tsp grated Parmesan
1 tsp (5 g) rolled oats
¼ cup (15 g) spinach, finely chopped
1 tsp olive oil

Cut the shrimps into small pieces. Mix the egg, cream cheese and Parmesan in a bowl. Stir the rolled oats, shrimps, and spinach into the egg mixture.

Heat the olive oil in a small frying pan, add the egg mixture, and cook on a medium heat for eight minutes. Turn and cook for a further two minutes.

Remove the frittata from the pan, allow to cool, and cut into small pieces. Serve a portion at a time.

THE CAT'S WHISKERS—FINE DINING FOR YOUR CAT

"LULU" CHICKEN AND TUNA SALAD

Makes 2 to 3 portions

1¾ oz (50 g) canned tuna (in brine)
1¾ oz (50 g) cooked chicken
½ oz (15 g) mixed salad leaves (e.g. radicchio, oak leaf lettuce, Boston lettuce)
⅛ oz (5 g) beetroot
1 tsp vegetable oil
1 tbsp plain yogurt
1 tbsp water
½ tsp freshly chopped flat-leaf parsley

Drain and flake the tuna. Cut the chicken into small pieces. Wash the salad leaves, shake them dry, and cut into very thin strips. Chop the beetroot. Place all the prepared ingredients in a bowl and mix.

In a small bowl, whisk the oil and yogurt with the water to make a dressing, and stir in the parsley.

Serve the meat and vegetable mixture a portion at a time, with some of the dressing drizzled on top.

RABBIT STEW

Makes 2 to 3 portions

3½ oz (100 g) rabbit
1 tsp olive oil
¼ oz (10 g) potato
¼ oz (10 g) chicory
¼ cup (50 ml) homemade chicken stock, see p. 8 (alternatively, dissolve ¼ tsp of additive-free vegetable stock powder in ¼ cup (50 ml) water)
¼ tsp chopped hazelnuts
½ tsp freshly chopped flat-leaf parsley

Cut the rabbit into small cubes. Heat the oil in a saucepan and brown the cubes of meat.

Peel and grate the potato, cut the chicory into thin strips, and add both to the meat in the saucepan. Add the stock and cook covered for ten minutes.

Remove the stew from the heat and allow to cool. Mix in the hazelnuts and parsley. Serve a portion at a time.

"MEOW" SHRIMP COCKTAIL

Makes 2 to 3 portions

2½ oz (75 g) cooked shrimps (without preservatives)
2 tbsp plain yogurt
1 tsp tomato paste
1 tsp vegetable oil
¼ oz (10 g) alfalfa sprouts
½ tsp freshly chopped flat-leaf parsley

Cut the shrimps into small pieces. Mix the yogurt, tomato paste, and vegetable oil together to make a sauce. Chop the alfalfa sprouts.

Mix the shrimps, sprouts, and parsley with the sauce. Serve a portion at a time.

POULTRY NUGGETS IN ASPIC

Fills three 3½ fl oz (100 ml) molds

1 tsp of granulated gelatin
1¾ oz (50 g) chicken
1¾ oz (50 g) duck
1 tsp sesame oil
7 fl oz (200 ml) homemade chicken stock, see p. 8
(alternatively, dissolve ½ tsp of additive-free vegetable
stock powder in 7 fl oz (200 ml) of water)
½ oz (15 g) iceberg lettuce
1 tbsp (10 g) cooked rice

Cut the chicken and duck into small cubes.

Heat the oil in a saucepan and sauté the meat. Pour in the stock and cook it for ten minutes.

Meanwhile, cut the iceberg lettuce into thin strips. Remove the meat from the stock, and mix with the lettuce and rice. Divide the mixture between the three molds (for example, empty foil catfood trays). Add the gelatin to the stock in the saucepan and stir vigorously until it is dissolved. Fill up the molds and place them in the refrigerator for three hours.

To serve one portion, loosen the edges with a knife. Dip the mold briefly in hot water and turn it out. Allow to stand at room temperature for 30 minutes before serving.

SALMON TROUT MOUSSE FOR LUCKY

Fills two 2½ fl oz (75 ml) molds

⅔ tsp of granulated gelatin
½ oz (15 g) zucchini
3 oz (80 g) salmon trout fillet
1 tsp corn oil
¼ cup water
1 tbsp low-fat cream cheese
1 tbsp whipped cream

Grate the zucchini, and cut the salmon trout fillet into small cubes.

Heat the oil in a saucepan and sauté the cubes of fish. Add the water and cook for five minutes. Remove from the heat, place in a high-sided container, and purée with a hand blender.

Add the gelatin and stir it into the purée so that it dissolves. Make sure the purée is very hot or it won't dissolve. Fold in the zucchini, cream cheese, and whipped cream. Divide the mixture between the molds and place in the refrigerator for three hours.

To serve a portion, remove the mousse from the refrigerator and carefully loosen the edges with a knife. Dip the molds briefly in hot water and turn it out. Allow to stand at room temperature for 30 minutes.

Liver pie

Makes two pies

1¾ oz (50 g) flour
1 tbsp (10 g) butter
3 tbsp cold water
3½ oz (100 g) beef liver
3½ oz (100 g) ground beef
1 egg yolk
½ tsp freshly chopped flat-leaf parsley
butter for greasing
flour for dusting
1 tbsp cream

Knead the flour, butter, and water together to make a dough, wrap in plastic film and leave to rest in the refrigerator for 30 minutes.

Wash the beef liver, pat it dry, and cut it into very small pieces. Place in a bowl and mix with the ground beef, egg yolk, and parsley.

Preheat the oven to 350°F (180°C). Grease two small tartlet cases or muffin molds and dust with flour. Roll out the pastry very thinly to make two circles, and use these to line the molds. Cut off any protruding edges, and fill with the meat mixture.

With the leftover pastry, roll out two circles the same size as the molds, and cut a hole in the center of each. Put the pastry lids on the pies and press the edges together. Brush the pies with the cream, and bake in the preheated oven for approximately 30–40 minutes.

Remove from the oven and allow to cool. You can feed your cat little chunks of pie as a reward.

Tip
The pies keep for a maximum of two days only in the refrigerator. It is therefore advisable to freeze the second pie immediately.

POULTRY HEARTS

Makes 2 to 3 portions

3½ oz (100 g) flour, plus extra for dusting
¼ cup (20 g) oat bran
2 tsp grated Parmesan
1 egg yolk
1 tbsp (10 g) butter
3½ oz (100 g) cooked poultry, puréed
(e.g. jar of turkey-based baby food)

For glazing:
1 egg yolk
1 tbsp cream

Knead the first six ingredients into a smooth dough. Wrap the dough in plastic wrap and leave to rest for one hour in the refrigerator.

Preheat the oven to 350°F (180°C). Remove the dough from the refrigerator and roll it out to about ⅛ inch (3 mm) thick on a floured work surface. Cut out small heart shapes with a cutter.

Line a baking sheet with baking parchment and lay the hearts on top. Whisk together the egg yolk and cream in a small bowl, and brush the hearts with this mixture. Bake in the preheated oven for 15 minutes.

Turn off the oven, open the door a crack, and leave the poultry hearts in the oven to harden. You can store the biscuits in an airtight container in a cool, dry place for 14 days. Make sure that they are completely cool and dried out and that they do not contain any residual moisture.

Picture credits
Corbis: 16 Don Mason
Getty Images: 1 Imagemore, 6 Peter Cade, 32 Brian Gordon Green, 44 GK Hart/ Vikki Hart, 56 Sharon Dominick